The Black Butterfly

Part 2

Pushing Through Adversity

RENEE MURPHY-CLARK

WESTBOW
PRESS®
A DIVISION OF THOMAS NELSON
& ZONDERVAN

WestBow Press books may be ordered through booksellers or by contacting:

WestBow Press
A Division of Thomas Nelson & Zondervan
1663 Liberty Drive
Bloomington, IN 47403
www.westbowpress.com
844-714-3454

ISBN: 979-8-3850-3016-3 (sc)
ISBN: 979-8-3850-3017-0 (e)

Library of Congress Control Number: 2024915444

Print information available on the last page.

WestBow Press rev. date: 10/22/2024

Contents

Dedication

I dedicate this book to the Spirit of Christ who lives breathes and resides all through me, preparing his people for a Kingdom not made by hands.

To my children and grands, I leave a Legacy for you to prosper as God sees fit.

2 Timothy 4:7
I have fought a good fight, finished my course, and kept the FAITH! Through it, I shall be triumphant through the love you all demonstrate after my passing to one another and others recognizing Christ is all you need to live a glorious life.
Love,
Mom

Dedication

...

Introduction

Pushing Through Adversity is the next part of "My Unfinished Story," which is my introduction to a world of soon-to-be clients and people who seek my advice, my introduction was to allow you to see that I am ordinary, for such a time as this!

Pushing through adversity is expressing the truth about our experiences and circumstances and facing them/our truth head-on!

Pushing through adversity is admitting we are born into sin and shaped by iniquity, Psalm 51:5; Surely, I was sinful at birth, sinful from the time my mother conceived me, (Palmer, 1995).

Pushing through adversity is expressing emotions and admitting to yourself and others that you are right or wrong! Or your opinion of a thing matters.

Pushing through adversity is when circumstances look like we are losing but, in the end, we win!

Pushing through adversity is telling ourselves no matter the circumstances we will achieve and be steadfast to conquer!

Pushing through adversity is the ability to cope

with loss, family dynamics, change, trauma, etc. the inevitable parts of one's life or events that bind/build the character of resilience.

Pushing through adversity means you can return to a place within your mental health capacity to be rechallenged and withstand again because we were never created to fail! Ephesians 2:10, For we are God's handiwork, created in Christ Jesus to do good works, which God prepared in advance for us to do (Palmer, 1995).

Pushing through adversity is being 15 years old and pregnant and wondering how you're going to survive along with this baby looking back over your life 39 years later saying I made it; we made it the baby and me! I never could have made it without Christ being on my side and holding my hand, but I did not know that then.

Losing a loved one who has always told you that this too shall pass you can do this wondering if they are sane. Finishing school on time and graduating, maintaining a job keeping a roof over your head is not easy at all mentally or physically when you are not proud but grateful for the roof. Rock bottom is how you must get up so things can change, you can change!

These acts are frightening when you are alone and scared because reality has set in. You have another life depending on you, party-over friends don't look at you the same, and people judge you in their silence, but the vibe is obvious because you wear your feelings on your sleeve not realizing it, sometimes on your face your actions talk to.

Taking your own life can and at times seems like your only option and then you wonder who will find and raise the baby. You tell yourself in that moment; No! not today, go eat and feed the baby do it all over again and again the next day.

Neurologically these drives, and urges, are secret battles playing outside our conscious awareness and controlling our thinking emotions, and behaviors shaping who we become.

We are so quick to psychoanalyze others by hiding who we are because we have psychoanalyzed ourselves to think we have it all in and under control. Not realizing we are out of control, and we are not talking about it demonstrating it in our opinions and behaviors of others, because lying is easier.

The noun Adversity: negative human actions, don't always have to be a person's outcome for change when we change our thinking process of how we view situations or circumstances we can triumph through life.

To triumph is achieving a victory, or positive outcome, being successful with every adversity one can overcome, and continue pushing through! Triumph is a feeling of great satisfaction and pride resulting from an adverse hindrance to achieving success or victory creating a successful ending to a struggle.

2 Timothy 1:7
The Spirit God gave us does not make
us timid but gives us power, love, and
self-discipline (Palmer, 1995)

Chapter 1

Put Your Name in the Prayer!

G OD'S GRACE MERCY AND PEACE ARE HOW THE songwriter puts it! I'm going to call it peace, which is a personal character trait humans create and implement growth for continuing peace when walking in your truth.

Peace is not necessary or important if you have never experienced adversity, chaos, or been in a situation where you have had your hands tied (figuratively speaking) and, in situations that are out of your control, chaos is necessary for humans to appreciate peace! Peace is a resulting end that most people want to achieve whether in death, business, politics, and personal relationships!

When we are at peace we breathe better, when we are at peace, we are resting in the thought of Godly principles that should govern our lives Philippians 4:7; And the peace of God, which transcends all understanding, will guard your hearts and your minds in Christ Jesus (Palmer, 1995).

To be at peace we must acknowledge who we are and at times if you know, through reading scripture whom we belong! Take a minute and think about your life and ask yourself what if this tidbit of information came out, Lord? What could this mean to me, my life, and maybe another person?

If you are reading this book guess what It is already out because whether you serve him or not your life was exposed when you did whatever it is, you have done. Proverbs 15:3; The eyes of the LORD are everywhere, keeping watch on the wicked and the good (Palmer, 1995).

True Believers in Christ already know this and if you say you believe in God and you live with secrets, because you are afraid of what it will do or the outcome, understand! It has already created a negative outcome because everything you live with is based on your judgment and that's the lie, we believe! Just because another human doesn't know makes you live a lie, because God knows!

Humans receive grace and mercy every day when we awake after resting to approach a new day, some of us are not teaching this fact to our children or people whom we care for in our homes or on our jobs, this is not always a spoken word but a way of life which represents how we treat others, this shows people we are at peace with who and what we are becoming or striving to be.

A new day starts in the dark, which soon comes to light and so does change at midnight a new day starts, and grace and mercy adorn us all with brand-new beginnings. God gives us promises in his word so call your name out or place your name in the scripture you need that brings reassurance and call God out on his word!

What brings me peace is the process of eliminating the unnecessary baggage that weighs me down, which I did not get to this thought process on my own, finding out in life that everyone has a purpose God allowed an automobile accident to catapult me into a direction that still needs grooming, learning things about myself and walking the road of life called Renee has placed me in the direction of counseling others to be better in the walk called them (place your name in a prayer).

The Lord is my Shepard, Renee shall not want, he maketh Renee lie down in green pastures, he restoreth Renee's soul, he leadeth Renee in the path of righteousness, (example). Watch how you feel after you have applied truth to your life! Truth is the word of God.

Another thing that makes or brings me peace is revealing my truth to others and showing them what surrendering it all to God looks like to me!

Which is the reaction on a person's face when I tell them I used to smoke crack cocaine or I smoked marijuana every day, or slept with a man for money, stealing from a store to feed myself or my children standing in front of my truth keeps the embarrassment of my past away, it was embarrassing when I was doing it but to be in front of my truth which is taking a stand and being responsible for what I have done keeps me in control of the narrative, God did that!

I am a walking talking miracle because when Christ knocked on my heart door, I opened it and tried him at his word, oh yeah, I tried him and today I'm so glad I did because momma and daddy can't always help us, but my walk-through adversity was purposed for me. I was made for the experience whatever it may be.

Being ashamed of my truth is what keeps me humble, for this reason, God can use me!

Proverbs 3:5-6

Trust in the LORD with all your heart and lean not on your understanding; v6, in all your ways submit to him, and he will make your paths straight (Palmer, 1995).

Chapter 2

Childhood Sundays

IT MIGHT SEEM STRANGE RUNNING BEHIND something that's already yours but that's when I found Jesus Christ, I had heard of him but never knew him as a healer, a way-maker, a protector, comforter, mind stabilizer, or Lord and Savior!

listening to the elders of the church I attended as a child, these are the names I heard when they referenced God or acknowledged worship during services on Sundays because I was made to go by my parents, however, I never really understood why they went because I grew up around some fighting arguing adults called mom and dad.

Today I understand all those names that I can recall because I use them myself and I understand the term of endearment as to why believers speak it. Oh, and because you were made to go to church my parents went, it wasn't always important to be saved, however, they always opened the doors of the church after each preaching session held, I still laugh at this.

Their parents made them go, and they were raising me with the mentality to go which also was a cultural thing for colored people to do anyway, go to church on Sundays even though you were at the club the night before probably still recovering from drinking, and some people still smelling like what they did! Smoking cigarettes in the back of the pew or the back of the church building in the parking lot. Through my eyes, I said I would never go to church after I had grown up and this is what I did, ran from the church because in my eyes and thoughts, why are half the people who are here, here?

I still laugh about this, but the perception of children should be monitored because my mind was exposed to conversations I heard in the restroom of the church and the back row of the pews, and living in DC you can run. Still, you can't hide because somebody always knew somebody in the city.

What I liked most of all on Sundays was dinner and changing my clothes at grandma's house after church, I met up with my cousins, aunts, and uncles we had a good time on Sunday afternoons, and my grandma expected us to always meet up at her house because soon as you hit the door to walk in the house the smells reminded you that grandma loved hard and deeply with having everything ready down to the dinner rolls, and desserts.

Oh, how I miss childhood Sundays at grandma's. Both my grandmothers were great cooks, one was an expert baker, and the other could cook anything right after killing it, I mean this literally.

Proverbs 24:27
Put your outdoor work in order, and get your fields
ready; after that, build your house (Palmer, 1995).

Chapter 3

Let Your Pride Seek Peace

I DID FACE CHALLENGES EVERY DAY BECAUSE OF the thoughts that moved through my head while trying to sustain myself, cope, and deal with the unknown because being in control of everyone and things in my view is how I thought I should live my life along with keeping quiet, speak when spoken too.

When I relinquished that control, I found an inner peace that surpasses all understanding of events and why things happened or happen to me as well as others. We think we are in control, which is really when we have lost control.

Wanting to be in control is a deceptive spirit that tells you, you need no one or you can do this by yourself, this is how pride slips in, and not that this is a wrong notion, but the enemy uses this to deceive us into thinking we don't need God! God bless the child who has his own; I get it, I agree, but if you have your own you have already been blessed.

Humans should only take pride in their convictions, appearances, and accomplishments and never get caught up in being bigger than their accomplishments because someone can be born who is greater than your accomplishment, humanity improves with every generation born or at least we are supposed to. Take pride in being a positive example!

I have seen many people in control and lose, and they had plenty, but to sustain humans must put God first in all things, God bless the child who has his own prayer life, worship, and mind to create fruit that lasts for generations to come.

Professional young athletes who make or sign contracts for millions of dollars become broke financially because of the lack of knowledge to sustain that flow. They cannot maintain financial freedom because they are ignorant of sowing financial seeds that produce more seeds.

When we as humans acknowledge God as our shepherd and relinquish our control to him, we make choices that should strengthen the mind and maintain our physical abilities to demonstrate to others that we are in control of our choices that create positive influences or environments where peace is always present.

Peace is an individual characteristic entity that we must tap into within ourselves, everyone around you can be in chaos, but you can maintain your peace and that's called being in control, when humans maintain their emotional state of being human.

Peace is an emotional state of mind! Peace is being in control, to be in control humans must be plugged into the creator of all things! Who is the God of our universe, peace is a place no one person can take from another unless you give it to them.

Humans should strive for peace daily too because in doing so we open doors no human can close or we close doors no human can open, making us free to move and breathe with ease. Let me express why this is of value to every human being because think of those moments when you are alone and you are at peace, it's quickly lived!

The phone rings, the kids are fighting, the spouse has an issue, folks outside your household want to come in from their chaos, you remember you forgot to pay a bill, or you forgot something! All this and more can steal or rob you of your peace.

When we allow things to disrupt our peace, we are vulnerable to all negative things. We feel like we are in control, and we can handle it until anxiety says here is a heart attack, stroke, or it is just out of your control.

Many of us don't like to wait and this is where our problems remain dormant, applying patience to every situation, and not allowing our issues to control how we live, move, and breathe is how we should be living.

Oh, the kids are calling, guess what they are going to always call my man is calling, he's going to call unless he's cheating, my friends are doing this and that, it is okay to be available. Still, you cannot allow things or other people to separate you from your peace, or "Peace of Mind," because God is in control and when he ties your hands you can't do no more than what he allows.

We are never in control, we are led or deceived into thinking we are, and someone reading this is still on the fence about this thought but guess what, you did not choose your birthday or the day you will die.

War is happening in the world as I write this book, and people are praying for peace in the Holy Land, and other places as well, but pray that the leaders who think they are in control can find peace within themselves (in their hearts) and this allows them to create peaceful environments. Finding common ground is where leaders should come together with the strength and power God has given them.

Mankind is at war within the human body everyday spirit vs flesh, Romans 7:22-25, For in my inner being I delight in God's law; 23 but I see another law at work in me, waging war against the law of my mind and making me a prisoner of the law of sin at work within me. 24 What a wretched man I am! Who will rescue me from this body that is subject to death? 25 Thanks be to God, who delivers me through Jesus Christ our Lord So then, in my mind am a slave to God's law, but in my sinful nature a slave to the law of sin (Palmer, 1995).

We free ourselves by what we think and believe, which can be beneficial to our health; when we are free, we are at peace! Free yourself! Jesus when amongst man on earth never rushed or made haste to heal or counsel his people but he did accomplish the "Will" of the Father, with all peace in his hands! Who is our example?

Romans 8:1-2
Therefore, there is now no condemnation for those who are in Christ Jesus, 2 because through Christ Jesus the law of the Spirit who gives life has set you free from the law of sin and death (Palmer, 1995).

Chapter 4

Looking ahead at your Legacy with Love

WHAT IS LOVE? LOVE IS STRIVING EVERY DAY to leave a legacy for the ones you care so deeply about, those who have meant more to you than your human-earthly desires, a legacy is a footstool to the next generation or family bloodlines, either created by you or those of importance to you, because not everyone has children of their own but we have people who mean the most to us.

Leaving a legacy is you living beyond death by creating footprints for living in a world you once visited in the flesh, God left us a legacy through Jesus Christ and when we create our legacy, we don't worry about death we look forward to the sweet transition of moving on to our great reward! Heaven is our reward, a street paved in gold means I am born to live beyond this world, but just like anything in life how will people know you existed without your legacy?

Love is leaving your footprint as an example to the humans that will come after us, love is living our truth because scripture tells us there's nothing new under the sun, meaning when we get to heaven we are new creatures, but on earth, you have to fulfill an obligation to self and that's being an example of how a person creates a legacy that speaks for you when you're gone.

A legacy is not about financial gain, it's about the message you learned and lived that made you unique for a purpose for which God created you.

We take care of our family because they are an expression of our love and the reason/meaning we were born to love and live. Make your purpose count for something other than folly. When your life has a meaning and you know it, Glory to God you are moving in and on purpose!

We should not be afraid or sad about dying or those who have gone on before us, because we know the truth about why they existed in our lives and why they meant so much to us as a member of a family or an individual experience because, without telling us they showed us and left a legacy that we understood was uniquely them.

In all things take your time to learn and this

includes grieving but don't linger, lingering opens doors that can create opposition, making for other adverse actions to be a part of your journey.

We are similar and sometimes we have the same names, but we are uniquely called, shaped, and blended, twins, triplets, quads, etc. we are uniquely different for God's purpose. Again, you may think you own your life, and you are in control, and there's nothing wrong with thinking but I'm here to tell you, you are not in control!

Sometimes bad things happen to good people and good things happen to bad people, the reason being is you are not in control! That's why you were in that place to see it happen or to be of comfort and witness the dynamics of human adversity.

"Pushing Through Adversity" is what we were created to do! The challenge is good versus evil, every day is a tug-a-war to live free from sin and God already knew we were going to fall, but he gave us help to get back up by sending Jesus Christ his only begotten son who is God in the flesh to be that ram in the bush for our salvation.

We die or should every day and yet we are not ready when it hits the life journey of a loved one, if we are to receive grace and mercy the way it was intended for us to get every morning then we must die to ourselves daily, with putting off the old and putting on a new mindset and the behaviors that create positive environments. It's like bathing, washing off the old smell creating a new clean smell.

If this was not a challenge to understand as people get older, think about it especially if you have done nursing older people don't bathe as much, I am not there but it happens ask a nursing home worker or a person who cares for the elderly, bath time becomes a hassle.

Walking with God daily means you are so occupied with learning new things about yourself and humanity that you create ways that bring about opportunities to change how we see death and why it is important to love beyond the grave, loving beyond the grave is living for a kingdom not made by hands.

And I know some are on the fence about this but understand you were created to love and live not to mourn! We mourn because we feel like a person's death was too soon or so unexpected, I am not trying to be heartless, I'm just trying to help someone see past what is inevitable, we prepare for births we should prepare for deaths, and we should talk more about it to our children so that they can value their existence and not take living for granted, it's not a video game there's no restart button.

Lord knows the hardest is burying children who have passed from illnesses, premature births, or senseless violence, the list goes on my heart goes out to people who have endured because you were created to handle a situation not all of us can.

1 Corinthians 15:55-57

"Where, O death, is your victory? Where, O death, is your sting?" [56] The sting of death is sin, and the power of sin is the law. [57] But thanks be to God! He gives us the victory through our Lord Jesus Christ (Palmer, 1995).

Chapter 5

Take Your Time,
Do It for You

G RIEF IS AN ACTIVE PROCESS OF COPING WITH A loss of any kind; however, grieving must be confronted, the reality of the loss, the emotional connection, and living to readjust, this is especially hard when we must accept death by unexpected occurrences.

Most counselors will probably call this ambiguous loss which refers to a loss that has no resolution or closure, or where small children are involved, and because people don't know this exists or refuse to find or seek help with a loss they are unaware of how if not dealt with, we have a society of angry humans walking around trying to live a life that creates moments of secret-depression.

If children are involved around the age of adolescence, they make it hard for the living parent to move on or cause disruption in a home because they have not had that physical closure causing what some counselors may call a stage of traumatic grief syndrome, which can occur for years until a process of healing has been initiated, if left unattended this process can emerge into adulthood with negative behaviors that follow.

As an adult, adults also suffer from traumatic grief syndrome. This truly depends on when a significant death has occurred and the age of the person who's experiencing the loss. Society doesn't allow humans to grieve at their own pace for fear of losing a job or not maintaining a lifestyle to which we have become accustomed, and our responsibilities we must not neglect. But what's important to a person who's grieving is giving them time to grieve with encouraging love-shoves that remind them they must live.

We must communicate about death because as people we can't get around it, but we must go through it, we do not collaborate well among fellow human beings sincerely when it comes to knowledge, relationships, and wisdom, I know this is difficult to some and others refuse to speak, and some fear but the best way to get through is to be equipped and ready.

We ready ourselves by placing our lives in order critiquing our generation and recognizing we don't know everything so that those we love and leave behind can transition also into a safe mental place that is psychologically healthy with having life insurance and speaking about final resting places which allow both parties involved to be at peace!

When people are placed in Hospice for whatever reason those staff members prepare the family and the one who's expecting to die, with creating information and the environment for a smooth transition so we must approach death and the subject to create a smooth transition by communicating a hard truth.

Some would say we have a paradoxical date with death, at times we are fascinated by it and what I mean is when people like Micheal Jackson died, or the Queen of England, Whitney Houston, and Aretha Franklin, we visit these places to see for ourselves and we walk away fine, but when it's a person that's close's to you we find difficulty in accepting death or the reality thereof, when we know this transition is going to happen whether we are ready or not.

Altering our attitudes about this topic we must open ourselves for the sake of generations to come learning that different generations have different mindsets and goals, their perception is not our perception because they live in their own time, and we of course live in ours.

I learned that the study of death is called thanatology which helps people deal with social attitudes toward death, bereavement, and grief. Suicide is a whole other issue and topic which is a sign of depression!

I do understand that different cultures have traditions, but families should discuss topics that are of vital importance and the preparations should be decided, no one anticipates children to die but according to the time in which we live today we must take precautions in our planning we are delusional to think otherwise.

I remember when a doctor told me I was going to lose my daughter at six days old and I refused to believe the doctor had the final say, I can only imagine when a mother miscarriage, or loses a child at birth after anticipating the arrival and the disappointment of not hearing the baby cry do to unforeseen complications, these types of situations need time to heal.

I am going to finish this grieving section because there might be some ramifications or disagreements about what I have to say and I'm not writing to hurt but to help others and self-heal from losses that go un-talked about because death is not a flaw it is purposed! Ecclesiastes 3:1-3.

I struggled with this section because I wanted to say what I had to say without leaving loopholes, meditation and pondering went into carefully selecting words that resonate and empower humanity to move forward when death approaches. God be the glory that everyone cherishes each day as though it's your last, no man knows the hour!

Matthew 24:36
"But about that day or hour, no one knows,
not even the angels in heaven, nor the Son,
but only the Father (Palmer, 1995).

Chapter 6

Coming Out as Pure Gold

S TEMMING FROM A NEED TO KNOW MY PURPOSE in life and dreaming of what could become of me while lying in a medical bed with a metal fixator attached to my left leg, I started to question God why me? Why was my birth important? Why is my name Renee, why are they my parents, why am I this messed up spiritually and physically with my leg dangling off and why would you fix me if I asked?

My purpose became clearer and even though it was mine I ran behind my purpose, it might seem strange running behind something that's already yours but that's when I found Jesus Christ, I had heard of him but never knew him as Lord and Savior because I was too busy running from him!

I never knew him as a healer, a way maker, a mind stabilizer, a protector, and a comforter so I had to be in a particular situation and experience something that changed my perception, thinking, and worldview of life on a level way bigger than I could have ever imagined.

While lying there in that hospital bed hearing and reading the story of Shadrach, Meshach, and Abednego I realized I was all three in one in a fiery furnace that was not just for me but for others to see who God is which showed me my purpose in life it is not about me which was hard for me to digest, it's about all of Gods people who have lost or never found their way to truth I had to be pruned and walk this journey because my will was of sinful-nature and pride and not of God. So being broken is what had to happen.

My attitude and how I saw others changed after and during my ordeal lying in a bed for eight months and hearing someone say the only way to fix me was to amputate my leg, but that was not God's plan for me, responding to my thoughts.

Daniel 3:17-18 If we are thrown into the blazing furnace the God, we serve can deliver us from it and he will deliver us from your majesty's hand, v18 but even if he does not, we want you to know your majesty that we will not serve your gods or worship the image of gold you have set up (Palmer, 1995).

Daniel 3:24, King Nebuchadnezzar was astonished and arose in haste he declared to his counselors did we not cast three men bound into the fire? (Palmer, 1995). Having seen a fourth person! I will trust God always.

Becoming a Master of Arts Clinical Mental Health Counselor means having the right attitude, spirit, patience having love embracing a professional lifestyle having a desire and a goal to fix a situation that can or could be fixed, and not overlooking people who need help.

Trusting God in his word declares that I will faithfully serve humanity by breaking barriers of change from cultural deception, integrating truth into people who only know sinful nature, (bad habits), and most importantly working with an ethical standard for the business of counseling. To be honest, this scares me, but I already do it.

Romans 12:6 We have different talents/gifts according to the grace given to each of us If your gift is prophesying then prophesy (Palmer, 1995) following your faith, and embracing a professional lifestyle does not finish after every graduation but ethics, accreditation, and credentialing are standards that need upkeeping, my goal is to run my facility so a commitment to the profession of counseling is a God-given talent where flourishing is not an option but a must do.

If psychology is the science that seeks to understand the behavior and mental processes of humans, then our approach to humanity must be distinguished involving accurate assessments of claims and making judgments based on supported evidence ethical guidelines promote the protection of psychological research and the highest standards for behavioral determinations of all clients I encounter.

I say this because being an advocate/ambassador for Christ means being a counselor in this present time is a special calling, I'm learning things about myself that confirm who and what my purpose is in the process of eliminating unnecessary baggage, and my perception of life has changed drastically.

Matthew 9:35-38

Jesus went through all the towns and villages, teaching in their synagogues, proclaiming the good news of the kingdom, and healing every disease and sickness. [36] When he saw the crowds, he had compassion for them, because they were harassed and helpless, like sheep without a shepherd. [37] Then he said to his disciples, "The harvest is plentiful, but the workers are few. [38] Ask the Lord of the harvest, therefore, to send out workers into his harvest field," (Palmer, 1995).

Chapter 7

From Caterpillar to Butterfly, Metamorphosing

I KNOW THAT WHEN THIS BOOK COMES OUT, I WILL have achieved my bachelor's in clinical counseling, a goal I have set forth and accomplished. Reaching for my master's I take pride in that walk and leap of faith because I assumed I was finished with school but now I can't seem to get enough of learning, however, scripture does tell us in all our getting; Proverbs 4:7, The beginning of wisdom is this: Get wisdom. Though it costs all you have, get an understanding (Palmer, 1995).

Metamorphosing is a process of all butterflies, and it's a process where learning and shaping take place not just in the body but the mind of humans also, we must metamorphose into new creations when we walk in the light of truth.

We cannot lean on what we think we know but we must lean on the facts as they present themselves to us, I have always heard that there are more female doctors (gynecologists) than any other type of medical doctor for men and children and this is because no two females are alike, and I believe this might hold but don't quote me! However, every life lived is uniquely made there are no two lives lived exactly alike.

People have tried but someone has had an experience that is different, but similar, to the next human being! At the age of fifty-five, I can say I have listened attentively for years to what people say, I don't always agree, and I don't always speak on it, but I have never heard someone say they can put on my shoes and your shoes and live your life. Clichéd you can try walking a mile in my shoes, but this is impossible for a reason. We are responsible for the walks we take and make in life, so why not show some accountability for what processes you encounter when you metamorphose into the person you become?

We must start to own our mess by acknowledging who we are and changing the things we don't want others to know, Micah 7:8, Do not gloat over me, my enemy! Though I have fallen, I will rise, though I sit in darkness, the LORD will be my light.

We cannot make people do what we want them to do, hence they have their own minds. We were created this way, and they just don't see a thing the way you see it!

Ask a comedian they see the humor in all of life even the stuff you don't, ask an archaeologist he can see structure in places you can't begin to think about building in, a hairdresser making a style with less creating more for the sake of self-fulfillment beauty.

This is not an easy process (metamorphosing) this takes time, to be honest, some caterpillars die in the process, however, most of the cocoons do make it, and the ones who die choose not to continue the process and have accepted defeat.

They are defeated because the comfort zone of being un-tangled brings fear when stepping out alone to grow. When humans process information, we do this as individuals until someone speaks to the group (the job of the black butterfly) and we still process it alone as individuals, if the information is processed correctly, we grow as individuals but when we come together, like in families, churches, organizations, forums, teams, and leagues we are on one accord, creating business. The lifespan is short because business is the priority of all the butterflies!

The information is preservation skills for living and

how we survive to stay alive! Humans are particular about what they (eat) want to feed themselves but open to what they feed their minds and for this reason, it is easy to accept defeat when the process of stepping out is a process of being alone.

We must make the process of stepping out ready for our offspring the next generation, why? It's the business! The business we aren't taking seriously, survival should be our focus not creating opposition for ourselves and our loved ones.

We create an opposition that allows for selfish gain and not generational wealth! The butterfly creates another path for the next generation to come live in after the generation in which it lives has passed on because the black butterfly covers the skills needed for survival and staying alive! We have children so that we can create generations that acknowledge God as the Creator! Or at least we should but we are out of focus.

Eve got out of focus in the Garden of Eden and the downfall or consequence she received was to endure pain during childbirth the first woman of all women, all suffer, an individual act can be a spiraling downfall for all! Persuasion trapped man. I am not blaming anyone simply saying there's nothing new under the sun, humans change, and God doesn't. His word the truth is written and is a guiding tool (Bible) for all of humanity when we are the reason the next generation is spiraling downward take a step back and see yourself as an individual who can change a generation which is everyone's calling.

With all the hate in the world we teach or allow, so many people can doubt me on this but when you laugh at the next person's dysfunction, their progress good/bad, or belittle them for who and what they look like or what they do or don't do, don't know, and misuse or ignore you have watered the plant called hatred.

I can't say it enough, not everyone thinks like you! This does not make them wrong; Micheal Jackson said and sang it best when he said, "I'm starting with the man in the mirror." We all should be checking and starting with the one in the mirror before we question anyone else.

Pride is a thing we must fix in ourselves before we find ourselves walking around pretending, we have hope, hence the need for more mental health counseling because we can't seem to get past ourselves, how we help or choose to deal with others should not be in a spirit of pridefulness or looking for something in return.

Matthew 19:24, Again I tell you, it is easier for a camel to go through the eye of a needle than for someone prideful/rich to enter the kingdom of God."

When we leave a legacy it's more than just money in the bank you leave a step up for the next generation to be better than the generation that's passing on, inventions, creative ideas for better ease of outcomes, and opportunities that some cultures are still trying to experience a creative craft that brings wealth.

Proverbs 13;22
A good person leaves an inheritance for their children's children, but a sinner's wealth is stored up for the righteous, (Palmer, 1995).

Chapter 8

Made for the Experience

REFLECTING ON MY ACADEMIC JOURNEY AS A professional mental health counselor and pondering the challenges and strengths based on my unique spiritual and physical abilities to endure, as a child my role model was Evil Knievel a stunt master in his profession.

In journalizing my development and discovery seeing my growth for the future I saw why my life took on certain turns and events that made me who I am today, I can say I am tough, but what makes me tough is the internal and external pain I endured growing up and experiencing in life as an adult going through challenges.

Life has not been easy, and I know I am not alone in saying this; however, life has been worth the pain endured not many will say this because I live a life of understanding and favor knowing I choose to keep my hand in the hand of the creator of heaven and earth.

A cancer survivor understands this meaning to the core of their existence as well as a true believer of Christ! Or to be fair a person who has had a close encounter with death.

The multidisciplinary study of how people change is not new, nature is a human development characteristic that changes throughout one's life.

I can truly say God has nurtured me and the calling placed on my life to be where I am today with a passion for helping others and implementing spiritual guidance through faith by showing people who I am and what they can be through counseling the misunderstanding to a place of understanding that the way we think and what we do is not new but challenging.

Genuinely, I am grateful for solidifying my professional identity and psychological understanding of why my calling is a mighty touch from the Creator because having compassion for humanity puts me in the "Will" of God meaning my life has meaning and purpose.

Like the Apostle Paul in scripture, Paul represents the will in a universal sense. Before Paul's conversion took place, he was Saul in the Old Testament, after his name changed along with his thinking process, he was called Paul obedience of the faith. This conversion took place in the Book of Acts.

Our present time demands that counselors be confident and steadfast in the faith or concrete in their learning because the scripture warns that the enemy walks around looking for those, he can devour 1 Peter 5:8, so if the enemy is doing this what must we as humans do?

Rest assured God has given us all we need to conquer our enemy, but we must submit our "will" to God's Will. Humanity (all kinds of people) say they believe in God but work in the darkness where they think others are not watching, and yes some of us are not watching because we know God sees all things and is in control of all things, knowing what carnal weapons you have in place don't work unless the Creator allows them too, read Romans 8: 7-9.

Romans 13:8 says let no debt remain outstanding except the continuing debt to love one another for whoever loves others has fulfilled the law (Palmer, 1995). I was made to attend church as a child and so on, a choice not given by my parents but chosen for me by my parents, I still laugh as I recall this memory. Someone reading this can recall such a time.

What our eyes see is not usually what we should internalize, however, what allows us to discover where and who we are is usually seen by the eyes, a significant part of what we discover is attached to a sense of emotional stability where we have landed in life during processes of development we sense a need to either push for what we want more of or walk away from what we think we don't want.

Security is an emotional state that stabilizes the thinking process in a place of feeling safe, we want to feel safe before knowing who or what we are, this thinking is complex and requires additional consideration of human nature.

Consider infants with their parents/caregivers, toddlers, adolescents, and teenage years when most of us discover the opposite sex/ or the same on a more physical level. We attach because of what we feel! Giving titles to people, places, and things, boyfriend, girlfriend, spouses, my favorite place, it's my good luck piece, using jewelry to denote a particular thing or occurrence, and this is normal in human existence.

But when do we recognize real security? The kind of security that people, places, and things can't provide. When people come to know Christ as their Savior, they are brought into a relationship with God that guarantees their eternal security.

Jude 24 declares, "To Him who can keep you from falling and to present you before His glorious presence without fault and with great joy." God's power can keep the believer from falling. It is up to Him, not us, to present us before His glorious presence (Palmer, 1995).

Our eternal security is a result of God keeping us, not us maintaining our salvation, so to live and breathe he creates us for every experience we have endured or will endure, scripture tells us he will not give us any more than we can bear 1 Corinthians 10:13.

I was eight years old when my uncle-in-law touched me in his upstairs loft in the barn and took my voice to speak about what was happening, over the years it created a rage that suppressed me making me an aggressive person, I could not tell the one person I knew that would have protected me and killed him, my DADDY!

Taking advantage of a child who was intrigued with his care for cows, bulls, and pigs was how the enemy lured me into that barn to take the very thing God is using me to do today, speak.

Dad informed anybody who was ever around us that if someone ever touched me or my mother for that matter, he would do what he said kill them I believed him.

But my uncle played on my childlike innocence by not wanting to lose my aunt who was my biological family relative of mine, my grandma's sister, and how I would destroy the family placing fear in me to remain closed mouth.

For years I never said a word, until I confessed it to a counselor, and in that moment, I got some of my voice back, but it had a tone of aggressiveness, two opportunities presented themselves for me to tell and a knot swelled in my throat causing me to tell a lie and say no.

The shock of what was happening created fear that I never knew being an only child my parents did give me a life of freedom. Everyone said I was spoiled because of how I was kept by my parents.

Nevertheless, this experience changed me, and I never wanted to go back to Beltsville, Michigan ever again, which is where I usually spent my summers, but I did go back and forth to Detroit, MI which is where my favorite aunt and uncle lived along with cousins and across the street from Hits USA now known as Motown.

My parents would fly and drop me off after a couple of days they would return to DC, and I would fly one-way by myself with a paid usher on the plane back home after my summer break was complete. Seeing a lot of superstars making music early in their careers who are famous to this day.

I brought this information out in chapter eight for a good reason; the number 8 represents material freedom, financial abundance and wealth, compassion, self-reliance, independence and freedom, confidence, inner wisdom, personal power, authority, professionalism, insight, and spiritual consciousness.

Which symbolizes infinite abundance, wisdom, and love 8 represents balance, introspection, intuition, abundance, ending a phase and entering a new life stage, being ready to receive change, and accomplishing goals related to business.

Today I am all this and more because of what I endured and what it tried to do to me, I was made for this experience! I walk in a newness of life and the Lord is my Shepard I shall not want, my soul has been restored, and he has prepared a table for me in the presence of my enemies, my cup runs over, and it is because I am obedient that surely goodness and mercy do follow me all the days of my life, Psalm 23.

Let's not get it twisted I do have bad days, but I don't linger anymore because God has made me able to withstand the bad and the good.

https://www.yourtango.com/self/angel-number-8-meaning

Psalms 24:1
The earth is the Lord and the fullness
thereof; the world and they that
dwell therein (Palmer, 1995).

Chapter 9

Decency and Order

HANDS ARE THE DEVIL'S WORKSHOP ACCORDING to Proverbs 16th chapter verse 27, raised hearing my whole life, however, all I seemed to do was injure myself as a child playing sports and doing every stunt, I saw on TV performed by my childhood Idle Evil Knievel.

Friday evenings after school, finish up my chores and outside it wasn't long before I had my parents sitting in an emergency room with a broken finger, hand, and wrist they were broken at the same time, today I used these hands to care for the elderly and my disabled daughter who lives with me as well as praise God.

Education is very important, no one wants to be around an airhead all the time, meaning education opens doors in life for opportunities to provide humans with more options, the more you know the more you grow! Plus, you have options to be diversified in life making every day more interesting. The brain is for housing intelligence.

When we learn new things on the job, they provide an in-service class giving you credit for learning more, so understand not everything is a paid college course all I am saying is to be willing to learn because things don't always stay the same. Grandma would say a hard head makes for a soft behind and this simply meant you are out of order!

1 Corinthians 11:3 tells us that the head of man is Christ, the head of woman is man, and the head of Christ is God! Perhaps showing us and giving us some perspective the head of a thing should bring order to its members in every aspect of life.

My Dad proved himself to be a provider, protector, and the dominating figure in the household he provided, and it was never lacking. Praise God, which means the example of a man I seek in life should be similar.

The heart is an organ that should be guarded spiritually and physically according to Proverbs 16:23, a wise man's heart guides his mouth. Webster defines the heart as a muscular organ that circulates blood by alternate dilation and contraction of the central vital or main part of the core, a place that feels emotions, and internal pain in your soul of existence.

Never commit knowing your heart is not in it -Nay! Keep your heart pure and never allow others to sway your thinking until there is proof, and check that too. Stand on your own and always give your word if someone can't accept your word don't do business, is the advice my dad pounded in my head as a child.

To summarize all that I have written here would be to say the heart, head, and hands of a person should follow up in whatever task/situation is placed before them whether in a good deed, pleasure, bad behaviors, or work, what's in the heart should be pondered in the head/mind for processing a task to the hands should perform a task by what's in the heart and mind of any individual, when people are angry their hands perform a task and when people are happy their hands perform a task.

When a person is angry a hand might want to hit another or use a gesture, or as we see today pick up a weapon, when a person is happy the hand may grab another to embrace showing love, do a good deed like open a door, clap for another accomplishment.

If you have a heart, mind, and the ability to use your hands you have all you need to make a difference in your life and the life of another human being! Make it count for something good! If you can't see this, I strongly advise you to seek righteousness, and ask the question why are you here? God is waiting.

Romans 3:23
for all, have sinned and fallen short of
the glory of God (Palmer, 1995).

Chapter 10

Real Beauty is Knowing the Truth

FORGIVENESS IS FOR YOU NOT THEM, BUT WE must forgive because we take back the very thing, they try to take from us, and forgiving them vengeance is mine says the Lord, Deuteronomy 32:35, It is mine to avenge; I will repay, In due time their foot will slip; their day of disaster is near and their doom rushes upon them" (Palmer, 1995).

The payback you may never know what it is but people who sow negativity do reap negativity before they leave planet Earth, Galatians 6:7, Do not be deceived: God cannot be mocked, A man reaps what he sows (Palmer, 1995).

We might not want to believe that, but it is true!

Anger fuels our motives and behavioral actions whether good or bad, humans harbor their anger/rage and think of vindictive ways to get a person back, like pranking/joking.

But not all actions are jokes, some can be very disturbing, causing others to lose their life or disrupt a person's way of life for moments at a time. If you're plotting on another human being, you might want to watch your back because God so loved humans that he created them.

God sits high and looks low for some reason we misplace this thought when doing wrong to one another, God is always watching, humans might not be watching but whatever you are doing can and will come out, you might think you're taking it to the grave but at your funeral, it came out.

You say to yourself who cares when I'm dead, well you should care because Matthew 18:18, "Truly I tell you, whatever you bind on earth will be bound in heaven, and whatever you loose on earth will be loosed in heaven (Palmer, 1995).

So, watch how you treat people and how you treat yourself because that's important also, everyone should have desires that make us unique and interesting to aid others who are of a similar mindset desiring peace and tranquility so that we may live lives worthy of a kingdom not made by hands.

Everyone should have a talent that's worth being

discovered in the environment in which people live for example in your community, because we are a useful kind of creation, and acting like crabs in a bucket mentality is immature to the very nature of humanity.

Preservation is the first law of nature, and we should always prepare ourselves never knowing when we might have to battle but a battle is something you fight when someone has defiled or violated your life or that of your family it's our job to protect ourselves heck it's our right to protect ourselves, family, family moral, values, and land if we must.

The time your life starts and the time your life ends let the moments in between those dates count for something! If God created me for his glory according to Isaiah 43:7, however, we know not everyone is called a believer or acknowledges being a believer, I am not talking to them because they can't hear me anyway, I write my books for people who believe in God.

Then why am I sad or why am I not as happy as I ought to be? I get it not everyone was dealt a good hand about who their parents are nor was the situation right, or as older people used to say I wasn't born with a silver spoon in my mouth.

Some people are born into their trauma, which is normal. I get it but we as believers who know and see this are accountable because it is our job to help and be examples of what we know is real! Luke 5:32, God did not come to save the righteous, but he came to save those who are now sinners to repentance (Palmer, 1995).

We have got to stop letting the enemy use us to be enemies to one another, we need to be helpers of one another, living our lives being free, setting examples of what reality and truth look like. Colossians 3:13, Bear with each other and forgive one another if any of you has a grievance against someone, forgive as the Lord forgave you (Palmer, 1995).

People who hide behind their lives are always keeping and telling secrets, secrets come with negative attachments to the truth, if you are ugly on the inside, you are always finding ways to beautify yourself on the outside, the truth is knowing real beauty radiates from within and that's a natural truth.

Hebrews 12:2
fixing our eyes on Jesus, the pioneer and perfecter of faith. For the joy set before him, he endured the cross, scorning its shame, and sat down at the right hand of the throne of God (Palmer, 1995).

Intermission Page

Psalm 33:9-12

For he spoke, and it was done; he commanded, and it stood fast.

[10] The LORD bringeth the counsel of the heathen to naught: he maketh the devices of the people of no effect.

[11] The counsel of the LORD stands forever, the thoughts of his heart to all generations.

[12] Blessed is the nation whose God is the LORD; and the people whom he hath chosen for his inheritance (Dr. C. Scofield, 1909).

Page intended for a moment of reflecting

Chapter 11

Anger and My Voice

I MENTIONED EARLIER I HAD A COUPLE OF opportunities to speak my truth but did not for fear of shame, and telling someone sooner, I feared what others would think, so glad that doesn't bother me today, however, it wasn't easy getting to this point, the courage I have today only God!

I am in front of what I do and it's more than just my choice I choose to make it the choice I ask God for daily to live a life he will back me up on if I make the right choice to live choosing him daily. I'm a winner in everything I do because my choice is choosing to be what You have ordained me to be Lord, sometimes that's being in a dark place to be the light a people so desperately need to see.

Sometimes it is being silent and sitting back and waiting for a particular person or a specific moment, I don't know until it has taken place, and trust me when I tell you it is not rehearsed sometimes, I am where I need to be to learn a thing or two myself. Sometimes the student is me!

But during these times we must be humble so that we may receive, don't become bigheaded with God. Hebrews 12:6-7, because the Lord disciplines the one, he loves, and he chastens everyone he accepts as his son," v7, endure hardship as discipline; God is treating you as his children, for what children are not disciplined by their father? (Palmer, 1995).

I remember teaching my children it's not what you do but how you do a thing, meaning have a reason but don't just do something if you have not given thought to the ramifications it could have, and when you do a thing make sure it's what you wanted to do and not what someone else wanted you to do.

Timing is everything with God we wait, and we wait to become frustrated and tamper with the business that we gave to God in prayer but because we can't see him moving, we create another problem that we must incorporate a solution for, causing us more stress.

Being loud, and being out front made me feel like I was visible being seen to receive the approval of others It made me feel like I was special and not dirty, I felt dirty because I had a dirty secret and that thing made me act a certain way, being an only child did not make it better, except for the nights I cried to myself, In my room knowing no one knew.

It was during those times in life I began to smoke weed more often during my childhood, losing myself in sports, I speak more about this in my first book, so I am not going to elaborate too much about this now, however, marijuana was a coping medicine method I'm not against it, but I do not need it today!

I am healed from my past or else I would not be talking about it today, the desire to smoke crack cocaine was another coping method that could have destroyed me BUT GOD!

Being promiscuous was not a coping method but I'm grown and can do what I want looking for love in all the wrong places moving or should I say spiraling downward, understand I was running from the truth like so many of us do rather than seeking help not knowing this kind of help counseling existed.

Getting in trouble in a variety of places with local law enforcement, petty crimes did not have to do jail time back then. To be honest, in my silence, I did a lot of walking away from the trouble I got into, lol. Praise God whom I was running from!

First real boyfriend relationship I got into, I used my voice, but I had a problem with relationships I never wanted to stay connected to a person for a long while, always moving and kept a job and a car after I got a little older, going to the club was my release on Fridays and Saturday nights.

I got a little older and maintained my first apartment after leaving home previously and staying with others first, when I secured my place, I did not allow anyone else to stay with me but my cousins only.

I was peculiar about being around other people. So peculiar I would always secure the nightshifts on my second job working as a nursing asst. in nursing homes and during the daytime I worked at Andrews Air Force Base where I took the civil service test GS-3 to secure that job straight out of Suitland High School. Worked alone always it was a quiet office and all anyone wanted to hear was a typewriter.

I had become what some counselors would say anti-social rage disorder, bipolar, and aggressive rage disorder. Well, they had to classify me because I was complaining to my OB-GYN about certain things and technology was not where it is today. The most obvious disorder that was prevalent at the time was bipolar, and they gave me pills for that.

It calmed me down, but understanding this made me keep my mouth shut again, and I never wanted to discuss my issues anyway it was just a fix that I had to take this medication twice a day. Never really fixing my problem.

Hostile is how I was described by my family and

close friends, for the most part, I was a loner too, this is and was my choice.

My advice to anyone is to speak your truth and never suppress it or live with secrets because you ruin yourself and the truth others need to hear which assures them, they are normal, scripture tells us there's nothing new under the sun, there's not an act of any kind a human can do that has not ever been done before.

If you can think of it, it has been done, good or bad!

Mark 9:24
Immediately the boy's father exclaimed,
"I do believe; help me overcome my
unbelief!" (Palmer, 1995).

Chapter 12

Reaching My Goals, and Achieving Them

MY MBA IS IN FRONT OF ME AND THE commission to head up the prison ministry of my church, and become a Notary in the State of Virginia, titles in which I take pride because achieving notoriety to be able to walk indoors knowing that obstacles are awaiting me God has already made possible with earthly achievements that Spirituality can over-achieve.

Sometimes you have to be qualified to be in the room, other times chance brings you in, but to be heard or even be considered one must be qualified to be in the realm of relevance.

Reflecting on my academic journey discipline

played a major role in completing each class and burning the late-night or early-morning oil that being thirsty for knowledge can give, the field of mental health is not an easy task when counseling others to be better.

Challenges and strengths based on my unique personal experiences hearing about others, and research have shaped who I am today, the multidisciplinary study of how people change is not new Ecclesiastes 1:9, What has been again, what has been done will be done again; there is nothing new under the sun (Palmer, 1995).

Whether we change by experience or change by choice, who we are is shaped by many complex factors of who and what we have experienced and then demonstrated.

I am genuinely grateful that solidifying my character means pursuing my education, with a psychological understanding of human behavior while gaining greater knowledge in the areas of human psychological nature/development.

This means relinquishing my control and perceptions to what it is God is showing and teaching me as an individual I don't always expect people to understand my point of view, however, I expect people to understand that their outlook is not what others see, everyone is entitled to their perception of a thing but if it's not working don't live there, change happens when we change.

We grow as certain biological and psychological brain matter develops with marking transitional phases from childhood to adulthood to becoming an older adult, mainly called life stages.

These life stages should bring about some clarity to just what human development should mean to us on a personal level and a shared level of concern for the next person, we define ourselves by the people we hang around the most, people who bring out the best in us, or worst.

Our thinking patterns should change with every birthday we encounter/or celebrate, I put it like this because there are people who don't celebrate their birthdays and this is because of negative experiences, depression, and or not having the people whom they want in their lives to celebrate with.

In theory, environments play a major role in how, what, when, or where people decide to engage in celebrations creating psychosocial balance to their development with an individual initiative and willingness to mingle with others, hence some family members don't mingle with other relatives.

When it's family it's usually materialistic reasons that govern most behaviors unless some type of abuse has taken place, financially some family members appear to have more than others and some feel embarrassed, or envious sad but true.

Children learn these behaviors early in school

by admiring what other students wear, and the type of shoes another wears, creating animosity amongst themselves. Placing pressure on parents to work harder to provide what they desire and to be all they want; is to be accepted!

After our high school years, our focus changes again and this should be to secure an occupation that provides for a lifestyle we would be comfortable maintaining if we are raising our children to survive! Because we know having an education or special talent is how a person succeeds financially.

The first major celebration that we honor as humans is high school graduation because it marks a transitional time in a young person's life! Unless the marking of your sweet sixteenth birthday is a cultural milestone in your family's dynamics.

We are only human, and survival is a part of all human nature and development, our senses tell us from within ourselves when we have approached, or a feeling of danger might be upon us if our eyes have not warned us previously and not everything is what it looks like.

Humans have a right to defend themselves and what they believe, so mind regulation is a human character trait that only an individual can initiate, suppress, or seek counseling for. Sometimes trauma detonates your perception of an experience, and you decide based on what you think may be right as opposed to what should be.

If you want better for yourself, don't complain do the work, if not get out of the way so others may do them, so many are a hindrance to us, family, and friends, by teaching them our negative ways when we should be allowing a person a fair shot at a great life.

Set some goals and achieve them on your time because that's what we have to answer for, what did you do with your time? Ask yourself this question and then change your narrative, by seeking God first because the impossible is only done by God.

Luke 18:27
Jesus replied, "What is impossible with man
is possible with God," (Palmer, 1995).

Chapter 13

Angry

ANGER IS A BASIC EMOTION THAT ENABLES A person to take defensive/ protective action to overcome obstacles and achieve goals in life-threatening situations anger is neither necessary nor sufficient for aggression, but it impels aggressive behavior overriding our self-control mechanisms in the brain.

Making humans aware of their emotions is a psychological issue that should be addressed when noticed. Some counselors call aggressive behavior a dysregulation stemming from suppressed anger that has remained dormant and silent for years and can be deadly from childhood if not caught into adulthood.

We as humans know that anger is neurological because we have seen people have seizures and nosebleeds and see red when asked what happened to make them so angry! Along with them not remembering the damage they might have done.

In my opinion, the silent angry person is the most dangerous of all humanity, long ago silent angry people used to be postal workers, (people would joke about going postal on others), and people who would walk on the job and shoot random people, or even those who don't deflect their emotions but become instantly hostile.

We must elevate our human understanding by continuing to teach children and adults that respecting others is not a thing of the past but something we must always maintain. Why are we losing respect for one another with no regard for human life?

We did not lose this overnight, and we won't regain it back overnight, but we must start somewhere with respecting one another's differences, and remembering what grandma said long ago, if you don't have anything nice to say then don't say anything at all!

Implementing self-control, and respecting self, and others is what should be our focus when we walk out of our homes in the morning for whatever reason. A new day produces new opportunities, new advantages or just being happy you're alive.

When you approach a person, it doesn't hurt to say hello! People need people, your life can change in an instant! You speaking to a person can determine if they help you If you find yourself in an unexpected situation, not just your family but speak to a stranger scripture tells us Hebrews 13:2, Do not forget to show hospitality to strangers, for by so doing some people have shown hospitality to angels without knowing it (Palmer, 1995).

The thought of entertaining an angel means God is in control and he loves me enough to allow me to approach an angel, angels can bless your life and the lives of those connected to you! Scripture also tells us to seek ye the kingdom first and all these things shall be added unto you! Matthew 6:33.

People are angry today for lack of being misunderstood and not being considered, humans aren't eating improperly what they are putting in our food at restaurants is causing biological chemicals in the brain to become deficient.

People are also hiding behind their truth, and when you are harboring so much baggage (drama), humans tend to become emotionally unstable.

We create these patterns of discord in our children who are already mimicking us by teaching them what they see us do, we teach fear, and intimidation tactics hiding behind technology not realizing having a conversation is the human connection we are missing.

PSA; Public Service Announcement

Why are we still driving and texting PULL OVER PEOPLE! Can't say that enough, JUST PULL OVER or let it wait until you can.

The transactional nature of a person's environment focuses on a person trying hard to maintain control of themselves or a situation, however, emotional experiences can reach a heightened level of awareness if not handled properly when engaging in the workplace, society, communities, families, and friends.

Suppose we do things with decency and order according to the scriptures 1 Corinthians 14:40, showing signs of past to future growth on levels of (spiritual) maturity, beliefs, values, and attitudes that produce quality fruit in our lives that flow into the lives of others, implementing and developing self-setting standards to our lives? The meaning of this would be self-respect.

If I have self-respect then I have respect for others, which also means I am setting the stage for others to act in a certain way choosing to be an example of what civilized humanity looks like. Now I am creating opportunities for myself and others because life will open doors because of my demeanor and not by what I look like.

I am not writing be make anyone seem or look naïve, all I'm saying is there is a race of people out here that don't see color as we used to see it, and it's called the mixed generation. Anger not only is an association of high stimulation of negative feelings and thoughts it also blames others by covering up emotions of fear and sadness.

White and black are no longer about to be a thing because according to statistics the Caucasian race is almost depleted, and people of color and every other nationality are mixing as well as the Caucasians.

God did that! When we mix, we have but one focus and that's survival, love, living, and not racing to be better than the next but preservation becomes the focus. More importantly, we must respect the race of people who are transgender, lesbians, bi-sexual, homosexuals, them and they.

Respecting one person is respecting all people, they did not create themselves scripture confirms that in 2 Timothy 3:2, People will be lovers of themselves, lovers of money, boastful, proud, abusive, disobedient to their parents, ungrateful, unholy, (Palmer, 1995).

Leave people alone and let them be who they are going to be, we are trying to take over God's job. Romans 8:28, And we know that in all things God works for the good of those who love him, who[a] have been called according to his purpose (Palmer, 1995).

2 Timothy 3:3-5
without love, unforgiving, slanderous, without
self-control, brutal, not lovers of the good, v4
treacherous, rash, conceited, lovers of pleasure
rather than lovers of God v5 having a form of
godliness but denying its power, have nothing
to do with such people (Palmer, 1995).

Chapter 14

DAD,

The Black Butterfly

MY DAD IS THE BLACK BUTTERFLY, MISSING him so much that I would advise anyone to read the first book I published. It gives an account of who my dad is. Finding joy at the same time as thoughts of yesteryear, reminiscing of the things I did not understand but understanding as time goes by.

My dad had anger issues stemming from suppressed trauma he experienced in his life, he suppressed his ordeal not realizing that one day it would consume him and make him into this intimidating, mean, and angry person. The "Jolly Green Giant" is what I called him.

With an eighth-grade education, my dad had to push through plenty of adversity being a man of color, and not having an adequate education, but what I admired most of all was his ability to humble himself to listen and learn whatever others were teaching.

It's not that he could not go to school it was because he had to work at an early age to help support his family, my grandparents were twenty-two years apart in age when getting married, granddad forty and grandma eighteen, when my grandfather died, my dad being the oldest boy had to maintain a job to help my grandmother feed a household of five children.

My dad was a truck driver which is what most of his jobs were, him driving. I knew my dad as a truck driver all my life. He worked at a paper company delivering big rolls of paper all up the East Coast until he brought his first chapter bus.

Dad learned at an early age the fundamentals of life and what was important for survival, because my grandmother was a maid and a good one because she had most of the homes in DC locked down, especially one family in particular.

As my dad got older and his siblings too, they knew what having a job meant, and going into the Army was my dad's next thing to do, so he went, and this became the beginning of my dad's psychological disorders.

Not only did our government overlook him but society as a whole overlooked, him because he was a waking talking person no one saw the inside scars that the Vietnam War created.

He was injured mentally and physically, we could not see it, however, he smoked cigarettes, he smoked weed, and he drank, I grew up with a bar in my home, plus my dad worked hard every day, a great provider, and he reverenced God! Not going to say he was saved yet, but he reverenced God.

My dad had traumatic events that he never spoke about, and I don't think we wanted him to, because he had nightmares (terrors) that could have hurt anybody if he had not come out of his sleep. He was hit in the knee by a ricochet from a rock fragment being hit by a bullet.

But emotionally my dad was overlooked because he was able to function but only when he was awake and having a good time, he was forceful in his stance of just being himself because of his height, and eventually his weight gain.

My dad wore a green uniform every day that he had cleaned on the job and pressed to perfection every week. The paper company required him to be neat and clean and in uniform every day, Monday through Friday, he represented the company well because they gave him his very own personal tractor-trailer.

The name Jolly Green Giant is what he reminded me of, and I was not the only one who thought so, other people saw my dad as a bully some said his stature was intimidating, but to know him would be to say he was honest and trustworthy, everyone referenced him like that.

To me, he was my dad, and he did not play when telling me to do something and do it to his satisfaction like my house chores had to be done a particular way and done right.

My dad was a prideful man he would beg the differ, but he was, he carried his self a certain way and he expected you to carry yourself in a certain way, don't walk behind him or in front of him looking like you had on hand me downs!

My dad was a name-brand guy, he wore expensive shoes, and clothes, jeans had to have a crease in the center, and a freshly pressed shirt on Saturday mornings, and his uniform was the same way.

My dad kept him a car and it had to be clean too, he never begged for anything, and you better not beg for anything either, he believed in giving and seldom receiving because he felt like he could afford all he had.

This also went for his nieces and nephews, as children we had more than enough around my dad, and he would get angry if you did not eat making sure you ate it all if he paid for it.

My dad was an attentive person he would recognize things before it was revealed, and he always observed his surroundings, I guess this was military skill, along with being in Vietnam, that place did a number on my dad when he talked about it, you knew never to ask questions just listen.

But I know this is where my dad endured trauma and this trauma was not revealed except in bits and pieces after he had hurt someone or something, he was very remorseful with every negative encounter, but it never changed the fact that he was a little damaged.

Asian Orange is what they treated most of the men for after returning from Vietnam and leaving the families to receive the benefit after each demise, but my dad died from a stomach cancer believed to be Asian Orange, the only thing the US government took credit for.

My dad did the best he could even though he was a little abusive when it came to disciplining me, I say a little because doing what he has taught and instructed has saved my life growing older and learning his ways has also made me a person I can respect, I had never seen him so humble as he was the week he passed away in the veterans' hospital.

I miss him and yes, I wish he had done things differently, but he was my dad, and I never was ever in want of anything, having more than enough all my childhood and we had good times too. Wishing I had told him my secret is all I regret.

Today I wonder what he would say if he knew I went to prison or even went back to school, became an Author, left D.C., became a Notary, a wife, a mother/

stepmother, and a grandmother, a woman who holds two degrees and pursuing my third MBA, and the leader of a prison ministry.

Rest In Peace Daddy, I love You! And the memories I have of you are cherished.

Chapter 15

Value of Life

B IBLICAL TRUTH PROVIDES HUMANS WITH THE value and assurance needed for living in a universe that God shaped and created just for us creating humans in his image Genesis 1:27, So God created mankind in his image, in the image of God he created them; male and female he created them (Palmer, 1995).

Revealing all possible truths the bible is still our guiding tool and should be used as a reference for providing Spiritual assurance that can make man elevate to realms of supernatural understanding and create more possibilities if only, he would seek first the Kingdom that is being prepared for all of humanity.

I have become everything that I have set out to be in this life but there are still things I would like to do while doing what I am motivated to do from Spiritual obedience, God called me into a place of obedience which means not my will but his will be done before I do what it is I think I want to do.

For instance, I never thought I would be someone's stepmother but I was called to do just what God wanted me to do, I never thought I would go to prison but had to do what I had to do, never thought I would be in a bad automobile wreck and survive but it has happened for reasons that created a better me or prepared me for greater.

We don't always agree, and we don't always like to go along but when we resist, we make things harder for ourselves, when we finally relinquish our will then things seem to fall into place by themselves without our interference, which is what usually complicates things anyway.

Being fondled and penetrated by my uncle was not my doing and I never thought anything of that nature would happen to me, but it did, to forgive him is something I had to do after he had died and I was grown, as a child forgiveness was not the issue or discussed because I never told anyone.

Today yes, I forgive him because the truth about why people hurt people is; that they are hurt! Now to be honest I did not care if he was hurt. What mattered most was what he had done to me! I wanted revenge and that revenge harbored itself down deep on the inside causing me to be a mean person.

Frustration made a home in the fiber of my being, people called me a bully and I thought that was cute, no one realized during those times I was fighting from within, I suppressed the pain of my experience to a place of making myself think it never happened.

I taught my children areas of their bodies that no one was supposed to ever touch without their permission and if they do, scream your head off, don't allow anyone to take your voice, raising my children with this mentality and never trusting them around anyone, my mom was my babysitter when I need one.

Many people's lives are ruined by fear, anxiety, and worry especially in times of adversity there is absolutely nothing you can do in your strength to solve your problems when the problem appears to be bigger than your abilities but tell someone who seems bigger than your situation.

As an adult knowing this truth and teaching our children early in life that God is bigger than anything we may encounter and he can handle every situation good or bad we endure, Philippians 4:7, And the peace of God, which transcends all understanding, will guard your hearts and your minds in Christ Jesus (Palmer, 1995).

Being ashamed and thinking, I was disgusting if I told or would my family mistreat me, were the thoughts that went through my head on a regular, it's not easy being an only child when you have endured an act of evil intent. But God!

God talks to us through prayer whether we are plagued by doubt or confusion whether we find it difficult to make a decision or not, praying can and will uplift and guide us restoring the balance to our lives and creating more value than when we first began, supplying us grace and mercy for every day!

I forgive not for him but for me! Genesis 9:6, "Whoever sheds human blood, by humans shall their blood be shed; for in the image of God has God made mankind (Palmer, 1995).

Genesis 9:5
And for your lifeblood, I will surely demand an accounting, I will demand an accounting from every animal, and from each human being, too, I will demand an accounting for the life of another human being (Palmer, 1995).

Chapter 16

Pushing Through Adversity

T HIS IS WHAT ALL OF HUMANITY MUST DO TO survive, we have life cycles we live through, challenges that come with age, experiences that we don't understand, and things we must accomplish just being human.

The teaching of civilization or teaching decency concerning our progress as humans, for instance, today I understand why past generations put the bathroom outside, not that I want it outside, but we understand why it was an outdoor facility.

Today we have a door and amenities to freshen an area that conducts a personal elimination process. Making decency and order a necessary behavior we

84

should teach our children and our children's children! This is the responsibility of all of us.

Pushing through adversity is praying for our leaders whom we are to obey because scripture tells us to or the consequences can be confinement, loss, or despair are all options, Hebrews 13:17. We like to think because we are a certain age we can do what we want but in actuality, we must do things that show we aren't harming ourselves or others.

You can do what you want but in moderation because excessive can cost you your life, and death for some physically and or spiritually creating health problems and side effects that we are never prepared for.

We have to teach the next generation how to maintain respect and decorum for self and others when raising them to be adults, having respect, because a person doesn't look like you, and having respect because a person's hair is not your texture.

Having respect, after all, some of us do pick up books and read them, having respect for cultural differences bringing about a variety of things that contribute to some of our communities that haven't always been but teaching our children to embrace diversity in ways we never thought we would and for some of us it's how we make it to the mountain top like Martin Luther seeing the dream of a whole new world we all want to be in!

Most importantly we as a people need to get the facts about everything before concluding things we know nothing about! Diversity is a thing that people of similar cultures and different cultures have trouble understanding when it comes to communicating our thoughts, needs, and wants.

We have plenty of mixed families in America and beyond, but we still have a problem with understanding that we are all human and we all want to be treated equally and respected, whether we identify with LGBTQ or straight, kids included.

Simply put the LGBTQ community is continuing to fight for rights because being human is not being respected, ask any woman in America or around the country because as a female we are still fighting, regardless of what is on the Law books.

The heart of a person who thinks they're in control or have the power to change a thing in our legislation is why we are still pushing through adversity in our communities and our states. We must pray for those who have ruled over us because they determine the outcomes of how we live amongst others.

What bills we pay, how we handle our everyday transactions, what technology they make available to us, and what we see and hear across our airways, governing our school's curriculums, designing the laws we all must live by, eyeballing your social media accounts which sometimes is not a bad thing, but you understand my point.

Meditate on the scripture reference!

Ephesians 6:12,
For our struggle is not against flesh and blood, but
against the rulers, against the authorities, against the
powers of this dark world, and the spiritual forces
of evil in the heavenly realms (Palmer, 1995).

Chapter 17

Relationships

CREATING AND FORMING RELATIONSHIPS IS human nature, we are made to create relationships, in other words, a relationship shows your regard for a thing, person, and place making it a noun that represents the state of being connected by employment for example (homeland), pet, marriage, immediate family, and ancestorial bondage.

Those of us who believe in God or have faith are considered in relationship with Christ, thus we call one another brother in Christ, sister in Christ! We have formed a relationship with a body of believers of similar faith.

Whatever your relationship status is it should be a connection that empowers you as a person, giving you insight, wisdom, and a helping hand through encouragement, supporting you in ways that aren't costly but idealistic, challenges, and motivation that push you to create inner strength to endure during your toughest adversity experiences.

In most of our relationships, we should want to give back and necessarily take all the time, scroungers exist, they are out there, and if you're not giving then you're one of them! Not all relationships are interactive, you don't get in bed with all your relationships! In relationships, we are submitting tithes and offerings unto God!

This is how we should look at what we do for others, not the giving of monetary as a means for all giving, Malachi 3, tells us about robbing God, we have robbed God if we are not serving our fellow man with insight to improving the (mental) state of humanity and this is not all monetary but being in a position to help another and neglecting to help makes you one who has robbed God.

For someone who has yet to understand here's an example; to cultivate the ground for gardening we must put forth an effort. This doesn't cost one thing but sweat and endurance, the harvest is plenty, but the laborers are few Matthews 9:35-38.

The black butterfly or the butterfly effect," derived from human chaos, the concept suggests small changes in one part of our thinking process which can lead to significant consequences elsewhere, remember, sometimes the smallest steps can lead to the biggest outcomes!

My advice to anyone is to be careful and consider carefully the relationships you form! Not all are beneficial, or healthy environments for you, your children, and others who are already in your circle. Ladies being beaten by your significant other this is not LOVE.

The person you are with might feed you, clothe you, and keep a roof over your head but if he/she is sleeping around, and not respecting you as a person he/she is not yours or worth your time place a value on your life and maintain it mentally and physically, love yourself first so that you can project genuine love to another who will return that same genuineness.

The word love is so freely being used today and what's being demonstrated is not love, but lust! No one can love you if they don't know you!

Christ-like love is to see a person in need and help them on their way and you walk away knowing you did something from kindness and from the love God has placed in your heart.

Philippians 2:5-11

[5] In your relationships with one another, have the same mindset as Christ Jesus:

[6] Who, being in very nature[a] God,
did not consider equality with God something to be
used to his advantage;

[7] rather, he made himself nothing
by taking the very nature[b] of a servant,
being made in human likeness.

[8] And being found in appearance as a man,
he humbled himself
by becoming obedient to death—
even death on a cross!

[9] Therefore God exalted him to the highest place
and gave him the name that is above every name,

[10] that at the name of Jesus every knee should bow,
in heaven and on earth and under the earth,

[11] and every tongue acknowledges that Jesus Christ is
Lord,
to the glory of God the Father.

Chapter 18

Wisdom At its Finest

PRESIDENT HENRY FORD ONCE SAID, "WHEN everything seems to be going against you, remember that the airplane takes off against the wind, not with it," (1947). I understand Mr. Ford's words to mean that adversity (being wind blowing against you) can make you successful and stronger by overcoming the challenge, thus triumphing.

My favorite wisdom writer Miya Angelou motivates me to always think critically about my future and the future of others. And it's because her thoughts resonate with me often.

Taking others into consideration is a prevailing reminder with an individual perspective, recognizing that all people cry, laugh, eat, worry, and die can introduce the idea that if we try and understand each other we can become acquaintances."

In essence, recognizing your unique experiences and respecting others' perspectives can lead to greater empathy and connection, which is what the world needs more of, kindness and consideration for the next person allowing the Spirit of God to open doors no man can close.

Isaiah 22:22, I will place on his shoulder the key to the house of David; what he opens no one can shut, and what he shuts no one can open (Palmer, 1995).

Galatians 6:3-6

If anyone thinks they are something when they are not, they deceive themselves. v4, each one should test their actions. Then they can take pride in themselves alone, without comparing themselves to someone else, v5, for each one should carry their load, v6 Nevertheless, the one who receives instruction in the word should share all good things with their instructor (Palmer, 1995).

Chapter 19

My Struggle Through Adversity

I HAVE SPOKEN ABOUT MY DAUGHTER PRIOR IN MY first book, she's a delight and a joy to receive every morning, and by the time this book comes out, she will be thirty-three in age, and still living with me in our home.

We will call her Dae for now; she has been disabled since she was six days old after contracting chicken pox as an infant in the newborn nursery of the hospital where I gave birth.

Dae has finished school and a variety of other educational programs; she's an excellent reader and she can't wait for this box to drop so she can read this one too.

She's never wanted anything because her mother is a go-get-her! Making sure her needs were met was a priority and still is, but for the most part she's older and I'm getting older.

But what I want to bring to everyone's attention is COVID-19 hit the nation and home health nurses were pulled from the home which was my ever-present help! I did not mind for a while, but a year went by and there was no change, another year went by and now I'm tired.

My daughter doesn't understand my exhaustion because all she knows is mommy's going to get me up every day of every morning and we are going to have fun and we will ride, or we will just hang out all day every day.

Not realizing the responsibilities of being a homeowner, a wife, going to school, and working were wearing me down, I could not pray enough for help or COVID to be over, to catch a break, or even just sleep through the night.

But what was happening was a process, I had to trust God for what he was creating in me to be in that moment and for today. Everyone who encountered us would say where's Dae because every time you saw me you saw her; I understood their concern, but they did not understand mine and the breaks I needed to maintain myself as her main caregiver.

When we are caring for a loved one, I would like to

think that we are caring for others also, we are giving them all of ourselves/attention from the heart to make sure they are comfortable and happy!

That being said, my daughter had no idea she was disabled because she was involved in everything we did as a family, and as a young adult we included her in our private moments, friendship gatherings from me, and my husband and to the children we brought to the marriage, Dae knows all our friends and enemies.

With me not getting a break ever she had to be passed around to the kids who are adults and stay home in her room which is her little apartment in my house with me in another room maintaining self-care to not burnout, family, or not caregiving is a job that should be rotated.

Psalm 121:1-2, I lift my eyes to the mountains where does my help come from? v² My help comes from the LORD, the Maker of heaven and earth (Palmer, 1995).

I prayed, I fasted, and I got depressed because I was tired, but it was in those moments God was working on my behalf, not just finding me any kind of help but finding me someone who would care for my daughter the way I would care for her, someone I could trust.

In becoming a counselor, I had to notice the absence of attributes like patience, determination, and distress that grow in us when we are unattended on levels far beyond what I thought these were.

Patience on a level when getting mad/upset/ornery

is not going to solve anything, and your problem is not everyone's problem so the magnitude in which I needed to be relieved was not what others saw, my determination as her mother to make sure my kid was well kept was not as important to others as it was to me.

I'm walking in distress which brings about depression, and self-loathing, becoming a counselor usually means you can relate to what others are going through or have been through.

The work the Holy Spirit was conducting in me was an overhaul of experience because the work I must do is to help others get through, not go around not getting by but how to make it through, even when it's a loved one who is the assignment!

God bless our nurses in this nation and all those who give of themselves so others can be comfortable, showing kindness regardless of the task. I commend you! May God forever bless you.

Jeremiah 29:11
For I know the plans I have for you," declares
the LORD, "plans to prosper you and not to harm
you, plans to give you hope and a future.

Chapter 20

My Goals and Accomplishments

IN MY LAST BOOK, I SPOKE ABOUT MY GOALS AND what I wanted to accomplish, and my readers you deserve to know my intentions going forward, I have completed all goals mentioned with completing my bachelor's degree and pursuing my master's to open my counseling services.

I also head up the Prison Ministry in the church where I fellowship, I have become a Notary in the state in which I live, and I'm also a certified Nurse.

I have more grandchildren and one on the way! God is good and he stays in the blessing business, I have celebrated twelve years of marriage by the time this book comes out.

I have been in a few automobile accidents to which God has been good because we don't look like what the car looks like. But we are still able to live our lives knowing that we walk, move, and breathe because of the grace in which mercy implores us to be.

I hope to open my counseling office after receiving all the licenses and certifications needed, and as God sees fit book three is being written titled "The Purging" which will be the last of this three-part series The Black Butterfly!

Most importantly thank you for your patronage and May God continue to bless you!

2 Peter 3:17-18

Therefore, dear friends, since you have been forewarned, be on your guard so that you may not be carried away by the error of the lawless and fall from your secure position. [18] But grow in the grace and knowledge of our Lord and Savior Jesus Christ. To him be glory both now and forever! Amen.

The End.

The End